Pennsylvania Railroad Company

Pennsylvania Tour to Mexico

affording four weeks in the land of the Aztecs

Pennsylvania Railroad Company

Pennsylvania Tour to Mexico
affording four weeks in the land of the Aztecs

ISBN/EAN: 9783337194673

Printed in Europe, USA, Canada, Australia, Japan

Cover: Foto ©Andreas Hilbeck / pixelio.de

More available books at **www.hansebooks.com**

PENNSYLVANIA TOUR

TO

MEXICO,

AFFORDING FOUR WEEKS IN THE LAND OF THE AZTECS.

BY A SUPERBLY-APPOINTED TRAIN.

———⊕

ROUND-TRIP TICKETS INCLUDE ALL NECESSARY TRAVELING EXPENSES.

J. R. WOOD,
General Passenger Agent.

GEO. W. BOYD,
Assistant Gen'l Passenger Agent.

PENNSYLVANIA TOUR

TO

MEXICO.

ˏ

———⊕———

" World wrongly called the new !   Thy clime was old
When first the Spaniard came in search of gold."

WHETHER, as many archæologists claim, Mexico and Central America hold the connecting links which alone will complete the broken chain of mythical information shrouded about the Rameses tombs and Aztec pyramids and temples, remains for time and intelligent exploration to solve. If not older than Egypt, certainly its ancient history is as prolific with legend and romance, and its story as fascinating as that of her elder sister (if Egypt is the elder), and when it goes back to the Aztecs and Toltecs and beyond, the narratives are as similar as are the pyramids, the temples, and the idols, and the aspect of cities with low flat-roofed houses spread upon a plain whose trees are feathery palms recalls descriptions of the land of the Pharaohs.

The Moor left his monument to Spain in the Alhambra, the Aztec his to Mexico in the pyramid at Cholula.

The American who travels has been a hunter after the antique as well as warm weather in winter, and when he could combine the two his journey was altogether a pleasure trip; he found them both in a mild way on the peninsula of Florida, but the old Castle of San Marco, at St. Augustine, was the most ancient ruin—in fact, was almost the only one ; the weather was warm enough, excepting an occasional " norther," and the territory of pleasure travel attractive though somewhat limited.   Gradually travel was extended to Cuba, and at last when the great railways to Mexico were completed a veritable Egypt of antiquities was found, and an Italy of sunny skies without crossing the seas ; tourists were content and their number increased greatly.

As to latitude, Mexico occupies the same position as Egypt—the Tropic of Cancer passes through both countries at their centres. But the comparison is in favor of Mexico. Although that country lies near and partly within the tropics, the high altitude of a greater portion where the lines of pleasure travel run is such that a perpetual spring time is the average of the weather, and while the traveler visits the scenes of the charming readings that have been his, he finds a clime to his liking, conducive at once to health and pleasure. Such

POPOCATAPETL.

travels can have but one result—a result that is apparent and goes without saying.

Under the Diaz Administration Mexico has fairly leaped to the front with progressive movements. It is now that tourists are directing their steps to this interesting land of the Aztec, Spaniard, and Indian.

It is decided, however, by one of the most experienced travelers and lecturers that the only proper way to journey through this country is by a well-regulated personally-conducted tour, and to this end the Pennsylvania Railroad Company has arranged this exceptional one.

A WORD ABOUT PENNSYLVANIA TOURS.

— —⊕— —

THE success of the Pennsylvania Railroad's personally-conducted tours to the Golden Gate and Pacific Coast points, which were inaugurated and run during the early months of 1891, induced the Company to announce not only a series covering the same territory for 1892, but also a tributary tour into that peculiarly attractive land of Mexico, replete with innumerable points of pleasure and health interest.

UNDER PERSONAL ESCORT.

The idea that pleasure travel, under personal escort, could be created and conducted by railroads originated with the Pennsylvania Railroad Company, and its development has demonstrated the truth of the claim. Since its inauguration the Tourist Department has steadily expanded. It has won and maintained the favor of the traveling public, by reason of the fact that large resources, an intimate and friendly intercourse with connecting lines, liberal rates, and superior equipment places the Company in a commanding position and enables it to operate this branch of its business on the highest grade of excellence.

The Pennsylvania Railroad Company is not unmindful of the fact that pleasure travel is increasing year by year. The American people are awakening to the realization that there is something to be seen on this continent and it is the purpose of these tours to provide the ways and means of gratifying their patriotic inclination in the most satisfactory, comfortable, and profitable manner, through the regularly appointed methods of travel, with only the addition of the supervising care of the Tourist Agent and Chaperon.

With this aim in view the Company has, during the past four years, conducted a system of pleasure tours that have been entirely unique in the history of such undertakings. It has been the endeavor of the management to surround its patrons with all the facilities promotive of comfort and pleasure that enterprise could suggest and capital provide. The trains have been reproductions of the best express trains, for which the Pennsylvania Railroad is justly celebrated ; the parties have been conducted by tourist agents especially selected for their ability and experience, and chaperons have been introduced as assistants to the tourist agents.

The Chaperon, a lady of culture and refinement, is charged with special care of the ladies. She not only ministers to their comfort in countless ways that suggest themselves to an experienced traveler, but has a watchful eye for those delicate attentions which might es-

IXTACCIHUATL.

cape the observation of the sterner sex. Ladies who would shrink from the idea of traveling alone may intrust themselves to her care with implicit confidence, as she will not only prove a companion, but will stand to them in that relation of protectorship which conventionality requires. While all the ladies will be the objects of her care, her especial charge will be those who are not accompanied by male escorts. No lady or party of ladies need hesitate for a moment to join one of these tours on account of the inability of husband or brother to act as escort.

The presence of the Chaperon removes every impediment that would deter a timid woman from undertaking a journey alone, and places them on a footing as independent as that enjoyed by the men.

In addition to the high-grade accommodations and entertainment in transit, the Pennsylvania tourists are treated with the same liberality wherever the journey is broken. The choicest rooms in the leading hotels are always reserved for their use, for which regular rates are paid, so that the guests, although members of a large party, enjoy all the privileges of individuals who may have made their own selections.

THE MEXICO TOUR.

It has been designed, in mapping out this tour, to cover a period of about four weeks for sight-seeing in Mexico, in which time to review her shadowy history of past empires and long-vanished races, her love of ancient splendor, her conquest, her people, and to visit all the principal points of interest. The tour will leave New York February 10th, 1892, running via Pittsburg, Cincinnati, Mammoth Cave, Birmingham, Montgomery, New Orleans, Houston, Galveston, and San Antonio; thence via Spofford Junction, Eagle Pass, and into the land of the Aztecs over the Mexican International Railroad and Mexican Central Railway, arriving at the City of Mexico on the afternoon of February 25th. Incidental visits will be made to Torreon, Zacatecas, Aguascalientes, Leon, Silao, Marfil, Guanajuato, and Queretaro. On Thursday, March 3d, the party will leave the City of Mexico for a few days' jaunt through the semi-tropical sections of the Republic, visiting Esperanza, Orizaba, Paso Del Macho, Santa Ana, Tlaxcala, Puebla, Cholula, and returning to the City of Mexico the following Monday morning, where a stop will be made until Tuesday afternoon before starting on the homeward journey. Returning, the tour will leave the City of Mexico Tuesday, March 8th, via the Mexican Central Railway, visiting Guadalajara, Aguascalientes, and Chihuahua *en route* to El Paso, where Sunday will be spent, and at a late hour that night the tour will leave homeward-bound, visiting Albuquerque, Santa Fé, Las Vegas Hot Springs, Pueblo, Colorado Springs (Manitou), Denver, and Chicago *en route*, arriving in New York March 21st. The rate for this tour will be $460.00 from Boston; $450.00 from New York, Philadelphia, and other points on Pennsylvania Railroad system east of Pittsburg; $445.00 from Pittsburg; covering every necessary expense during period absent.

HOW THE TOURISTS TRAVEL.

The train for the conveyance of this party to and from Mexico has been constructed by the Pullman's Palace Car Company especially for this service. It will consist of a Composite Smoking Car, a Dining Car, Drawing-room Sleeping Cars, and an Observation Car, all of the latest Pullman Vestibule pattern. In fact, it will be an exact counterpart of the world-renowned PENNSYLVANIA LIMITED, which, by universal verdict, is the handsomest and best-appointed passenger train in existence.

A brief sketch of the cars in the order in which the train is made up will serve to give a faint conception of its magnificence.

The Pullman Vestibule Composite Car is exclusively a gentleman's car. The forward end is set apart for baggage. A compartment introduced into this car is fitted up as a barber-shop and bath-room. A regular barber's chair and all the paraphernalia of the tonsorial artist are at hand. He shaves the subject with an ordinary razor, and accomplishes his task as deftly as if his shop were stationary, instead of having progressed say fifteen miles between the lather and the brilliantine. A bath-tub occupies one side of the compartment, and the hot and cold water which fills the tub may be tempered to the taste of the bather. Adjoining the bath-room there is a refreshment compartment, from which a white-jacketed attendant may dispense exhilarating beverages in response to the tap of an electric bell.

The main portion of the car is a smoking-saloon. It is finished in natural wood, furnished with comfortable rattan arm-chairs, a lounge, a sofa, and two writing-desks, each surmounted by a small case of selected books. The upholstery is rich, but substantial, and well in keeping with the purposes of the compartment. Broad plate-glass windows, slightly bowed, admit a great volume of light, and reveal to the occupants a panoramic view of the passing scenery. In this, as in the other cars of the train, handsome chandeliers of nickel or brass depend from the roof, fitted with gas-burners and electric-light bulbs. Apart from the stationary lights there are also movable electric lights attached by insulated wire to the sides of the car, capable of being shifted to any position desired by the user. Their convenience in reading or writing is inestimable, as one may shift the light to suit his position. This admirable arrangement originated with, and was introduced into practical use by, the electrical department of Pullman's Palace Car Company.

A DELMONICAN DINING CAR.

The Dining Car is not only a dining-room in which forty people, disposed at ten tables, can dine in the most comfortable manner, but it contains a kitchen in which four cooks can prepare meals for thrice the seating capacity of the car, a storage-room for the provisions, ice-chests for wines, china-closets, linen-lockers, and the entire outfit of a large restaurant. The kitchen at the forward end is equipped with four ranges, on which every variety of cooking is easily done. The most skillful housewife would hardly believe that so much work could be accomplished in so contracted a space, yet by the economizing of every inch and the ingenious employment of every device that cunning minds could originate, the purpose of the dining car is achieved most successfully.

The dining-tables are fixed in the body of the car, and accommodate four persons each, allowing ample room for the service of a meal in courses. Glistening silver and glass-ware vie in brilliancy with the spotless linen, and above the tables, in the spaces between the windows, potted plants are placed on shelves set in the hard wood. The interior of the car is bright and cheerful in finish and decoration, and no odors of the kitchen are noticeable within the dining-saloon.

A conspicuous advantage of the dining car, and one that is appreciated most highly by all long-distance travelers, is the regularity with which meals are served, and the liberal time allowed for taking them. The serving of breakfast or dinner is not dependent on the arrival at a designated meal station, nor is the limit for consuming it confined to the dyspepsia-breeding period of twenty minutes, but between fixed hours the meals are ready, regardless of where the train may be, and one may tempt a perhaps capricious appetite as free and untrammeled as to time as if he were seated in Young's, Delmonico's, or the Bellevue.

The hours for meals will be observed as follows :—

Breakfast	7.00 to 9.00 A. M.
Luncheon	12.30 to 2.00 P. M.
Dinner	6.00 to 7.30 P. M.

LUXURIOUS SLEEPING QUARTERS.

The Pullman Vestibule Sleeping Cars composing this train are the best examples of nineteenth century car-building. They each contain twelve sections of two double berths, and two drawing-rooms, containing two double berths and a sofa. Inclosed toilet-rooms for ladies and gentlemen occupy separate ends of the car, and in addition the drawing-rooms are equipped with private toilet attachment. A distinct species of wood is employed in the finish of each car, and each possesses an individuality of its own in the coloring of upholstery and the tint of the drapery. The ornamentation of these cars is elaborate, though tasteful. The hard-wood finish is handsomely carved, and the exposed surface of the upper berths is inlaid with delicate tracery, or covered with appropriately-tinted embossed velvet. The several chandeliers, which might equally as well be termed electroliers, hang in glittering clusters from the roof-ridge, and at night shed a mellow radiance over the exquisite workmanship which they illuminate. Movable lights are attached to each section, so that one can lie in one's berth and read, with the light disposed as best suited to the reader's convenience.

In one of these cars there is a bath-room for ladies, fitted in every respect as if it were attached to a lady's chamber at home. It is supplied with hot and cold water, as well as all the accessories of the toilet. A lady's maid is in attendance, ready to serve one's bidding, and always on the alert to anticipate the wants of the passengers.

A PANORAMIC VIEW OF THE ROUTE.

By large odds the most popular car in the train, and one which exemplifies the latest development of transcontinental travel, is the Observation Car, which brings up the rear. Its interior presents a revelation in car-construction. The body of the car is an open sitting-room, finished in hard wood, and furnished with rattan arm-chairs and sofas. Among its conveniences are a writing-desk, a library of selected books, movable tables, and one of Blasius & Sons celebrated upright pianos, which cannot fail to prove a source of much pleasure. The daylight streams through handsome plate-glass windows, and at night the incandescent lights, both from the overhead electroliers and the movable globes, serve to thoroughly illuminate the interior. The rear door is composed of plate-glass from its top to within two feet of the floor. The rear platform is deeply recessed, so as to form an open observatory. The protecting sides of the car and the overhanging roof shelter its occupants while they sit and enjoy an unobstructed view of the scenery.

OBSERVATION CAR.

The platform will accommodate about twenty people in camp-chairs. This car is for the free use of every passenger.

In the forward portion of the main saloon sits a stenographer and typewriter, ready to take down and transcribe, without charge, the thoughts of the tourists for transmission to friends left behind. This feature has never before been presented on any train in the world except the Pennsylvania Limited and Golden Gate Tours, and it will undoubtedly commend itself to the appreciation of the tourists.

The entire train will be heated by steam and lighted by electricity generated by the dynamo or drawn from the storage batteries.

No other train has ever intersected this wondrously picturesque home of the Aztecs so perfect in its appointment, and no regular traveler can secure such accommodations as are offered to the Mexico Tourists by the enterprise and liberality of the Pennsylvania Railroad.

BAGGAGE.

A baggage car, in charge of Pennsylvania Railroad Company's baggage-master, will be attached to special train, and tourists may have access to baggage therein throughout the entire trip. One hundred and fifty pounds of baggage will be allowed on each whole ticket, and seventy-five pounds on each half ticket. Special tags will be furnished each purchaser of tickets, one of which, bearing name and home address, as a ready means of identification, should be attached to each piece of baggage to be checked, and such baggage checked by tourist to Cincinnati, the first halting point. These checks will be collected by the special baggage-master on train. After checks have been delivered to the special baggage-master tourists need give themselves no further concern regarding baggage, as all necessary transfers and rechecking will be attended to.

At Eagle Pass, on the going trip, and at Juarez, returning, the customs officers will board special train for inspection of luggage. They are very polite and their duties quickly performed.

SOME HINTS.

American gold always commands a premium, and bank drafts are in demand. The rate of exchange may not be quoted here, as it is constantly changing, but it is usually from thirty to forty per cent. The currency most in use is silver, but bank notes are in circulation among those able to own them. Some of the paper money is not accepted beyond the limits of the States where issued, but the notes issued by the Banco Nacional and those of the Bank of London, Mexico, and South America are good anywhere. For every-day use silver is recommended.

The metric system is the legal coinage, but instead of speaking of cents the number of *reales* is named in giving prices, *dos reales*, twenty-five cents ; *cuatro reales*, fifty cents ; *seis reales*, seventy-five cents ; and *un peso*, one dollar. The smallest copper coin is a *tlaco*, one and one-half cents, except the *centavo*, one cent piece ; a *cuartilla* is three cents ; a *medio*, six and one-fourth cents ; a *real*, twelve and one-half cents ; a *peseta*, twenty-five cents ; a *toston*, fifty cents ; and a *peso* is a dollar. The gold coins are seldom seen, the *onza de oro* is sixteen dollars ; the *media onza*, eight dollars ; the *pistola*, four dollars ; the *escudo de oro*, two dollars ; the *escudito de oro*, one dollar.

Change is made to a nicety, and if the line divides a *tlaco* it is cut in two with a hatchet.

With such clothing as is used in the United States for spring and autumn wear, a winter tour of all Mexico may be made. If the journey is extended through the "hot country" on the coast, and if any stay is to be made, summer clothes will be most comfortable.

DETAILED ITINERARY

OF

PENNSYLVANIA TOUR THROUGH MEXICO.

———:‡———

TUESDAY,
FEBRUARY 9th.
Leave Boston in Pullman sleeping car, attached to the Boston and Philadelphia night express, New York and New England Railroad Station (Summer Street), 7.00 P. M., Worcester (via Putnam) 7.40, Willimantic 9.40, Hartford 10.45, Meriden 11.27 P. M. ; New Haven 12.01 midnight, Bridgeport 12.35 A. M. ; arrive at Philadelphia 6.40 A. M. following day. Breakfast in the Broad Street Station restaurant. Remain in Philadelphia until 10.30 A. M. Wednesday, when the special train is due from New York.

WEDNESDAY,
FEBRUARY 10th.
Tourists will leave New York, Pennsylvania Railroad Stations, foot of Cortlandt or Desbrosses Streets, by special train of Pullman vestibule drawing-room sleeping, dining, smoking and library and observation cars, at 8.20 A. M. ; Brooklyn (via annex boat, foot of Fulton Street) 7.30 A. M. Arrive Philadelphia, Broad Street Station, 10.30 A. M. Leave Philadelphia, Broad Street Station, 10.40 A. M. and traverse by daylight the magnificent garden spots of Pennsylvania to Harrisburg, which will be left at 1.40 P. M. From here on the ride will be over the famous Allegheny Mountain region, the Horse-shoe Curve, past the

(14)

ill-fated Johnstown, and reach Pittsburg 8.30 P. M. Eastern time becomes Central time at Pittsburg, and watches should be set back one hour. The night and early morning will be passed *en route* to Cincinnati on the Pennsylvania Lines.

THURSDAY, FEBRUARY 11th.

Arrive at Cincinnati, the "Queen City," over the Pennsylvania Lines at 6.30 A. M., where the day will be spent in reviewing places of interest, prominent among which are the Art Museum in Eden Park, and the noted Zoological Garden. Numerous attractive drives well repay the time in taking. (See page 27.) Luncheon and dinner will be served at the Burnet House, corner Third and Vine Streets, and at 11.30 P. M. Cincinnati will be left, over the Louisville and Nashville Railroad, from same station at which tour arrives. Sleeping cars open at 9.00 P. M.

FRIDAY, FEBRUARY 12th.

At 7.00 A. M. Glasgow Junction will be reached and breakfast enjoyed on the dining car. From here, at 9.00 A. M., tourists will leave by regular train for one of the most delightful side-trips to Mammoth Cave, which will be reached at 9.40 A. M. (See page 27.) Luncheon will be served at the Cave Hotel. Leaving Mammoth Cave at 4.00 P. M. they will reach Glasgow Junction at 4.30 P. M., and embark on their special train at 5.00 P. M. via the Louisville and Nashville Railroad for Birmingham, Ala. This twilight ride through the historic Southern fields is not without its interest, but soon the gray tints of the approaching night will enshroud the fast-flying train, and not until early Saturday morning will Birmingham be reached, where several hours will be spent sight-seeing.

Leaving Birmingham at 12.30 P. M., the tourists will arrive in Montgomery at 4.00 P. M., where three hours will be profitably employed in visits. (See

**SATURDAY,
FEBRUARY 13th.**

page 28.) Leave Montgomery 7.00 P. M. The run over the Louisville and Nashville Railroad from Montgomery will enable the tourist to arrive in New Orleans early the following morning. The party will remain in their home on wheels, which will be side-tracked at a convenient point on Elysian Fields Street and used during the stay there.

**SUNDAY,
FEBRUARY 14th,
and
MONDAY,
FEBRUARY 15th.**

In New Orleans. (See page 28.)

**TUESDAY,
FEBRUARY 16th.**

Leave New Orleans at 12.00 noon via Southern Pacific Railroad through the "Louisiana low lands" and Texas. Almost immediately after passing through Algiers (the Jersey City of New Orleans), the way leads through the famous rich sugar lands. Vast reaches of canefields come into view, peopled with groups of sable laborers, the monotony of the horizon is broken by the planters' homes, and large *ingenios*, or sugar-mills, at frequent intervals. On speeds the train through long aisles of submerged forest land, moss-draped and gloomy, where, now and then, drowsy alligators, disturbed by the intrusion upon Nature's quiet, roll sluggishly into the black waters.

**WEDNESDAY,
FEBRUARY 17th.**

Arrive at Houston 3.00 A. M., after a run of three hundred and sixty-two miles from New Orleans, and proceed via Gulf, Colorado and Santa Fé Railroad at 4.00 A. M. on a side trip to Galveston, which will be reached 7.00 A. M. Visit points of interest covered by carriage ride, included in ticket. (See page 30.) Leave Galveston at 2.00 P. M. for Houston, which is reached again at 4.00 P. M., and six hours will be devoted to sight-seeing (see page 29) ; leaving at 10.15 P. M. via Southern Pacific Company. The run west will be taken up again during the night for San Antonio.

Arrive at San Antonio 7.00 A. M. Here a drive about the city and visits will be arranged to the Alamo, the Government Post, and the Missions. (See page 30.) Leave San Antonio at 1.00 P. M. for Eagle Pass, which will be reached at 6.30 P. M., and after crossing the Rio Grande to Ciudad Porfirio Diaz, **THURSDAY, FEBRUARY 18th.** where a short halt will be made, and then leave via Mexican International Railroad. The entrance is made into Mexico at this point, but ere the next stop is made tourist will be gliding along through the State of Coahuila 'neath the shadow of Mexican mountains. At Eagle Pass Central time changes to City of Mexico time. Watches should be set back thirty-six minutes.

The section of Mexico first traversed is an arid and unproductive region, although here and there through the valleys are found fertile spots—oases in the desert. Nothing of particular scenic interest or importance is lost to the tourists in making a large part of this trip in the night.

At 11.00 A. M. Torreon will be reached, and one and a half hours' stop will be allowed, where enough of interest will be found to occupy profitably the time. (See page 31.) Leave Torreon at 12.30 **FRIDAY, FEBRUARY 19th.** P. M. via the Mexican Central Railway, its main line extending twelve hundred and twenty-four miles from Juarez to the City of Mexico, this distance not including its branches, and over its entire length the tourists travel before again reaching the domain of the United States, the line from Torreon to the City of Mexico being traveled twice. As the journey is continued southward from Torreon along the borders of the States of Coahuila and Durango, the route nears the mountains. During the night the train, by a succession of tortuous windings around a mountain, reaches an elevation of over eight thousand feet above the sea level, and Zacatecas is at hand.

Tourists will arrive at Zacatecas at 3.00 A. M., and remain all day to visit the points of interest (see page 31), and enjoy a side trip by tramway to Guadalupe. Leave Zacatecas 4.00 P. M.

SATURDAY, FEBRUARY 20th.

At Zacatecas Station there is no sign of a city, but when the train leaves the passenger will get on the left hand a full view of a city of seventy-five thousand people a hundred feet below. With its low, flat-topped houses, and here and there a domed church, one could easily be persuaded that the scene was laid in Syria rather than in our western hemisphere. The train winds around the mountain side, keeping the city in view for several minutes. During this part of the trip the rear platform of the observation car will be an especial coign of vantage. Before Zacatecas fades from view Guadalupe appears, and the scene presented is one of marvelous beauty ; in the distance Lake Pevernaldillo is discernible. Enough of daylight will be left to show the rich agricultural character of the country and the beautiful fertile valleys *en route*. Arrive Aguascalientes at 8.30 P. M.

SUNDAY, FEBRUARY 21st.

At Aguascalientes. (See page 33.) Visit alameda, hot springs, and baths. The train will be located at the station, about one mile distant from plaza, which is reached by tramway.

MONDAY, FEBRUARY 22d.

Leave Aguascalientes, via Mexican Central Railway, at 3.00 A. M. and arrive at Leon at 8.00 A. M. Thirty miles from Aguascalientes the train crosses Rio Encarnacion on a lofty bridge one hundred and fifty feet above the stream, which flows through a deep ravine. Prior to reaching Encarnacion the route enters the State of Jalisco, one of the Mexican Pacific Coast States, and the only one touched by the party while in Mexico. The city of Leon is one of the chief manufacturing centres of Mexico, with a population of upwards of one hundred thousand, and its chief industry is in leather goods. Tourists will have time to take the tramways to the plaza, and likewise visit the cathedrals. Leaving Leon at 1.30 P. M., still on the Mexican Central Railway, Silao will be reached at 2.30 P. M., where all the points of interest may be reviewed. (See page 34.) At 9.00 P. M., via the Guanajuato Branch of the Mexican Central Railway, the special will leave for Marfil, which will be reached at 9.45 P. M., and the sleeping cars will be utilized for the night's rest.

MONDAY, FEBRUARY 22d.

In the morning, tramway to Guanajuato will be used in reaching this "quaintest and most delightful spot under the sun." (See, for description, page 34.) Thus the whole of Tuesday will be spent in sightseeing at Guanajuato and Marfil ; the latter point may be reached any time during the day, and at 11.00 P. M. Marfil will be left via the Mexican Central Railway and Silao reached at 11.45 P. M. From here on the route is very attractive ; the country for the most part is a fertile agricultural one. The culture of *pulque* may be seen in the great fields as the train speeds on to Queretaro.

TUESDAY, FEBRUARY 23d.

At 12.30 A. M. the run will be made to Queretaro which point will be reached by 7.00 A. M., and the remainder of the day until 11.00 P. M. spent in sightseeing. (See page 36 for description of city.) The train will be the home of the tourists.

WEDNESDAY, FEBRUARY 24th.

Leave Queretaro at 4 A. M., and run in a southerly direction to the City of Mexico, which will be entered at 1.00 P. M. After leaving Queretaro the train passes through the noted Hercules factory village with its tropical groves, then the great stone aqueducts, on through San Juan del Rio, the plains of Cazadero, down through the Tula Valley, and on through the cut which opens at Huehuetoca, reveal-

THURSDAY, FEBRUARY 25th.

ing the first view of the snow-capped mountains, the volcanoes of Ixtaccihuatl and Popocatapetl, and the plain of Mexico.

FRIDAY, FEBRUARY 26th. In the City of Mexico.

SATURDAY, FEBRUARY 27th. In the City of Mexico.

SUNDAY, FEBRUARY 28th. In the City of Mexico.

MONDAY, FEBRUARY 29th. In the City of Mexico.

TUESDAY, MARCH 1st. In the City of Mexico.

WEDNESDAY, MARCH 2d. In the City of Mexico.

During sojourn in City of Mexico carriage drive will be taken around the city, and short excursions to the suburbs, so as to cover all important points of interest.

During the stay in the city tourists will be located at Hotel " Iturbide " for sleeping accommodation, and their meals will be served at a neighboring café. (See page 36 for descriptive matter of the City of Mexico.)

THURSDAY, MARCH 3d. Leaving the City of Mexico at 12.00 noon via Mexican Railway, the road runs due north three miles alongside the causeway to the village and church of Guadalupe. Continuing farther, on the right-hand side can be seen Lake Texcoco, the city, and volcanoes of Popocatapetl and Ixtaccihuatl, which latter are scarcely out of sight during the remainder of the day. One hour after leaving City of Mexico the Pyramids of the Sun and Moon appear on the left. They do not strike the beholder as very majestic, but in reality their dimensions are quite imposing, being two hundred and ten and one hundred and fifty feet in height respectively. After a ride of fifty miles the plains of Apaur, the great *pulque* district, are reached. For miles on either side long rows of *maguey* plants, the source of this national beverage, may be seen growing. Esperanza is reached at 5.00 P. M. Tourists will remain in the sleepers over night.

From Esperanza, which is left at 7.00 A. M., the train will speed on through the most delightful scenic country. In a few minutes *Boca del Monte* is reached, where the down grades begin at a height of seven thousand eight hundred and forty-nine feet above the sea, and roll to Maltrata, a point only five thousand five hundred and forty-four feet, making a descent of two thousand three hundred and five feet, and taking sixteen miles of track to reach a point immediately below and in sight all the time. The little patch of tiled roofs and church with its dome of red, to be seen far below in the valley, is Maltrata. An idea may be formed of the windings of the road in making this descent when it is told that the Indians selling fruits and flowers at the little station about half-way down will leave by path through the cañon and reach Maltrata before the train arrives, and embrace another opportunity for the disposal of their wares. The scenery is beyond all description, and the trip will never be re-

FRIDAY, MARCH 4th.

gretted nor forgotten. From Maltrata the road follows the Rio Blanco through the valley of *La Joya*, the jewel, and Orizaba reached at 9.30 A. M. (See page 44.) Orizaba will be left by special train of coaches over the Mexican Railway at 10.30 A. M., and Paso del Macho reached at 12.30 P. M. This run will give a very desirable opportunity for viewing the scenery from Orizaba on, as the track lies on the mountain side, winds in and out in sharp curves, through tunnels, over bridges and along ledges where the cañons are hundreds of feet deep, and coming to the Metlac gorge crosses it on a curved bridge, which may be seen with the track on the other side of the gorge for some minutes before from the right-hand windows, and far below is a foaming torrent rushing down the *barranca* under the arches of an old stone bridge of the public highway. Leave Paso del Macho, returning, at 12.45 P. M., and arrive at Esperanza 7.00 P. M. Retire on train. (See page 44.)

SATURDAY, MARCH 5th.

Leave Esperanza via Mexican Railway at 3.00 A. M., and reach Santa Ana (via Apizaco) at 7.00 A. M., where a transfer by tramway will be made to the ancient city of Tlaxcala to visit the palaces, cathedrals, and many points of interest. The return to Santa Ana will be made by a tramway, thence the run will be made over the Mexican Railway to Puebla, which will be reached at 1.00 P. M. At 2.00 P. M. a side excursion will be made to Cholula, returning to Puebla same afternoon. (See page 46.)

SUNDAY, MARCH 6th.

In the City of Puebla, the train being the home of the tourists. (See page 47.)

MONDAY, MARCH 7th.

Leave Puebla 2.00 A. M., arrive City of Mexico at 9.00 A. M. The rest of the day will be devoted in the City of Mexico, where the train will be the home of the tourists until the following afternoon.

TUESDAY, MARCH 8th.

Leave City of Mexico via Mexican Central Railway at 2.00 P. M. for Guadalajara, which will be reached at 11.00 A. M. Wednesday.

WEDNESDAY, MARCH 9th.

In Guadalajara. (For descriptive matter see page 48.) This city will be entered by a branch line of railway extending from Irapuato westward. The road traverses the valley of the Rio Lerma, one of the most populous regions of Mexico, passing through a number of towns, the chief of which, La Piedad, has ten thousand inhabitants. La Barca, thirty-nine miles farther, is nearly as large. Near Ocotlan the road crosses the Rio Grande de Santiago, not far from its outlet into Lake Chapala. This lake, although near the line, is not seen from the cars. It is the largest body of fresh water in the republic, being sixty miles long and about fifteen miles wide. It is bordered by the States of Michoacan and Jalisco. Stop will be made at El Castillo Station *en route* to Guadalajara, in order to permit visit to the Falls of Juanacatlan, reached by tramway.

**THURSDAY,
MARCH 10th.**

In Guadalajara. Leave at 7.00 P. M.

**FRIDAY,
MARCH 11th.**

Arrive Aguascalientes at 7.00 A. M., where four hours will give ample opportunity for a second visit to baths and other points of interest. At 11.00 A. M. the journey will be continued to Zacatecas, where the train will arrive at 2.00 P. M., but as this point was thoroughly explored in the south-bound trip the train will speed on over the scenery previously passed in the night.

**SATURDAY,
MARCH 12th.**

At 1.00 P. M. Chihuahua will be entered. (See page 49.) At 7.00 P. M. this old town will be left in the rear of the fast moving train in its journey through the picturesque region on to El Paso.

**SUNDAY,
MARCH 13th.**

Arrive Juarez at 7.00 A. M. and El Paso 7.30 A. M., Mexican time, where there will be a stop over Sunday. (See page 51.) Tourists will retire in the cars, as the special train will pull away from El Paso at 9.00 P. M., Mountain time, twenty-four minutes faster than Mexican time, over the Atchison, Topeka and Santa Fé Railroad.

**MONDAY,
MARCH 14th.**

Arrive at Albuquerque at 7.30 A. M. Leave Albuquerque at 8.00 A. M., and arrive at Santa Fé 12.30 P. M. (See for descriptive matter page 51.) Leave Santa Fé over the Atchison, Topeka and Santa Fé Railroad at 3.30 P. M. Arrive at Las Vegas Hot Springs at 7.30 P. M., and locate at Hotel Montezuma until luncheon the day following. (See page 51.)

**TUESDAY,
MARCH 15th.**

Leave Las Vegas Hot Springs via Atchison, Topeka and Santa Fé Railroad at 3.00 P. M., for Pueblo via Trinidad and Denver and Rio Grande Railroad, which will be reached

**WEDNESDAY,
MARCH 16th.**

At 2.00 A. M., and left via the Denver and Rio Grande Railroad at 2.30 A. M., Colorado Springs (see page 52) will be reached at 5.00 A. M., where breakfast in the dining car will be taken and then tourists will be located at "The Antlers." All day Wednesday and Thursday morning at Colorado Springs to visit Manitou and Garden of the Gods, included in carriage ride covered by ticket.

THURSDAY,
MARCH 17th.

Leave Colorado Springs at 12.00 noon over the Denver and Rio Grande Railroad for Denver, which will be reached at 2.45 P. M., and the remainder of day devoted to sight-seeing, including carriage ride provided by ticket. Dinner at the Hotel Windsor or The Albany. Leave Denver by the Burlington and Missouri River Railroad at 11.30 P. M.

FRIDAY,
MARCH 18th.

En route through Northern Colorado and Nebraska to the World's Fair city. At McCook, Neb., Mountain time changes to Central time—one hour faster.

SATURDAY,
MARCH 19th.

Arrive Chicago, via Chicago, Burlington and Quincy Railroad, at 9.00 A. M. Breakfast on train, and transfer to Auditorium Hotel, where the party will be located during sojourn in Chicago.

SUNDAY,
MARCH 20th.

Two days for a visit to the various points of interest in the city, including the parks, the site of the Columbian Exposition, and stock-yards. Leave for the East by the Pennsylvania Lines at 4.00 P. M. (Central time), on the Pennsylvania Lines through Indiana and Ohio.

MONDAY,
MARCH 21st.

Over the main line of the Pennsylvania Railroad, through the celebrated scenery of the Allegheny Mountains, along the Conemaugh Valley, by the new Johnstown, around the Horse Shoe Curve, and through the Juniata Valley by daylight. Eastern time east of Pittsburg, one hour faster than Central time. Arrive in Philadelphia 4.00 P. M. and New York 6.20 P. M. The New England tourists will use the Boston Express leaving Philadelphia, Broad Street Station, at 6.20 P. M., after supper at the restaurant, arriving in Boston early the next morning.

Round-Trip Rate from Boston $460 00
Round-Trip Rate from New York 450 00
Round-Trip Rate from Philadelphia 450 00
Round-Trip Rate from Pittsburg 445 00

(The New York rate will apply from all other points on the Pennsylvania Railroad system
east of Pittsburg and north of and including Quantico, with proportionate rates
from points west of Pittsburg on the Pennsylvania Company's Lines.)

Tickets will be sold for children between the age of five and twelve years from Boston at $385.00, from New York, Philadelphia, and Pittsburg at $375.00, if separate Pullman accommodations are required ; or from Boston at $325.00, from New York, Philadelphia, and Pittsburg at $315.00, if they share the berths of parents or attendants. These rates include, in addition to round-trip transportation and Pullman accommodations (one berth), all meals, hotel accommodations, carriage rides, transfers, and side trips as outlined in foregoing itinerary, as well as services of interpreters. The rate from Boston includes, in addition to above, Pullman accommodations (one berth) Boston to Philadelphia and return, breakfast going and supper returning at Broad Street Station, Philadelphia.

DISTANCE TABLE.

	MILES.
New York to Cincinnati	757
Cincinnati to Mammoth Cave	210
Mammoth Cave to Birmingham	312
Birmingham to Montgomery	96
Montgomery to New Orleans	320
New Orleans to Galveston	415
Galveston to Houston	53
Houston to San Antonio	209
San Antonio to Torreon	552
Torreon to Zacatecas	267
Zacatecas to Aguascalientes	75
Aguascalientes to Leon	105
Leon to Silao	21
Silao to Guanajuato	15
Guanajuato to Queretaro	100
Queretaro to City of Mexico	143
Side trip over Mexican Railway	510
City of Mexico to Guadalajara	380
Forward	4,540

	MILES.
Forward	4,540
Guadalajara to Chihuahua	999
Chihuahua to El Paso	225
El Paso to Santa Fé	339
Santa Fé to Las Vegas Hot Springs	90
Las Vegas Hot Springs to Colorado Springs	275
Colorado Springs to Denver	75
Denver to Chicago . . . . : . .	1,025
Chicago to New York	912
	8,480

RATES FOR EXTRA PULLMAN ACCOMMODATIONS.

Each ticket entitles passenger to one double berth in sleeping cars for the round trip (except in the case of children occupying accommodations with their parents or traveling companions, for whom separate rates are quoted), but extra Pullman accommodations can be secured at the following additional charges :—

Entire section for one person	$80 00
Drawing-room occupied by one person	210 00
" " " " two persons	130 00
" " " " three "	60 00

NOTE.—It should be borne in mind that the above are the *total* charges for use of drawing-rooms, and that the *per capita* charge for two persons occupying drawing-room is $65.00, and that for three persons the *per capita* charge is $20.00.

DIRECTIONS FOR FORWARDING MAIL.

On or before Friday, February 12th, to New Orleans, La.

On or before Saturday, February 13th, to Menger House, San Antonio, Tex.

From February 14th to 28th, to Hotel Iturbide, City of Mexico, Mex.

From February 29th to March 7th, Post-office, El Paso, Tex.

From March 7th to 10th, to Hotel Montezuma, Las Vegas Hot Springs, N. M.

From March 11th to 13th, to "The Antlers," Colorado Springs, Col.

From March 14th to 17th, to The Auditorium, Chicago, Ill.

All mail should be addressed in care of Tourist Agent Pennsylvania Tour to Mexico.

Descriptive Outline Sketches

OF

INTERESTING POINTS *EN ROUTE*

AND IN MEXICO.

———⊕———

CINCINNATI, O.

757 miles from New York.

Beautifully situated on the north bank of the Ohio River, covering two plateaus gradually rising from the river, are the homes of the inhabitants forming the Queen City of Cincinnati. The prosperity of the place has been phenomenal. Along the river for over ten miles the business houses and residences extend. Covington and Newport, Ky., on the opposite bank, are connected by fine suspension bridges. The buildings of Cincinnati have a decided air of solidity and comfort about them. The drives are numerous and very attractive, and the museums and gardens, the Tyler-Davidson Fountain, the Suspension Bridge, and the noted Zoo Gardens will repay visits. The chief industries of the place are pork-packing, brewing, and the manufacture of boots and shoes. These institutions all warrant a visit, and the push and activity of the near West is illustrated in the life and business whirl of this place.

MAMMOTH CAVE, KY.

967 miles from New York. 210 miles from Cincinnati.

This cave, in which a distance of two hundred miles may be covered in following the numerous natural twists and turns, is undoubtedly one of if not the most interesting in the world, outrivaling even the one of Adelsberg in Austria. It is filled with grottoes, labyrinths, abysses, weird carved echoing chambers, streams, cascades, and lakes. The temperature in the cave is almost equal all the year. The entrance to the cave proper is very picturesque, leading down a steep rocky gorge. The tourist will pass through the Rotunda, along Audubon's Avenue, view the Little Bat Room, the Giant's Coffin, the Star Chamber, the Fairy Grotto, the Echo River, and a hundred other such strange and fascinating points of interest.

BIRMINGHAM, ALA.

1279 miles from New York. 312 miles from Mammoth Cave.

Few points in the New South manifest such marked growth in material prosperity as this exceptionally-located city of Birmingham. At its doors are the rich fields of ore begging for release and the most fertile agricultural land in the South. Its recent prosperity, in a great measure, is not alone due to the fever of "booming," but may be traced to the great railroad facilities it enjoys.

MONTGOMERY, ALA.

1375 miles from New York. 96 miles from Birmingham. 320 miles from New Orleans.

Montgomery, the capital of Alabama, will ever be famous as the first capital also of the Confederate States (from February to May, 1861). Its name came from General Richard Montgomery, who fell at Quebec. Prominent places of interest worthy of visits are the United States Court House, Post-Office, City Hall, County Court House, and the State House. Scores of interesting suburban points will reveal to the Northerner what typical Southern life is.

NEW ORLEANS, LA.

1695 miles from New York. 320 miles from Montgomery.

No city in America remained for such a long period of years so distinctively foreign as New Orleans.

Clustering about its early life hang some of the most thrilling events in history, while all that bespeak the inimitable gallantry of the French, the passionate love and hatred born in the Spanish, and the strikingly brilliant race of Creoles, have given it a peculiarly individualized and original people, of whom Northerners know little or nothing and find hard to approach. This is only their exterior, for underneath burns the hospitable courtesy of the most earnest sincerity, that trait for which Southern entertainment and hospitality have justly received such renown.

Nowhere else in the world will such varied and novel sights be seen as along Charles Street. In a short walk is the old "Cathedral of St. Louis," located between the old court-houses, where all the executions took place. Two or three blocks farther down Charles, back of a high stone wall, is the archiepiscopal palace. A few steps from the palace and one enters the St. Mary's Chapel, where the Archbishop often holds service. On the corner of Hospital and Royal Streets is one of the old-time palatial houses, under whose roof the nobility and famous were entertained.

Down Royal Street toward Canal may be seen the high art of exterior decoration, as displayed by the olden-day architects, particularly demonstrated in the projecting balcony windows with carved stone work. Between Royal and Bourbon is the Academy of the Bon Secours on Orleans Street. This convent was the dance-house of the theatre, and a ball and supper-room, and here were given the famous "quadroon" balls. Down Royal Street, at the corner of St. Peter, is one of the oldest and most notable houses in the city, owing to its being the first four-story house erected in New Orleans. Just back of Congo Square, where long ago the negroes danced and sang their strange, wild, weird songs, is the Parish Prison. The "marble-room" in the Custom-house on Canal Street is well worth a visit, as it is pronounced one of the largest and handsomest rooms of any public building in the country.

General Jackson's headquarters were at 84 Royal Street, and the old battle-ground of 1815, in St. Bernard Parish, is now "Chalmette," a national cemetery. These places mentioned above should be visited as well as the principal points, such as the Lake Pontchartrain, Spanish Fort, Metairie Cemetery, Carrollton, the Jockey Club, the French Market, and Under the Oaks, the famous dueling ground.

HOUSTON, TEX.

2057 miles from New York. 362 miles from New Orleans.

Houston is an important railroad centre, and a point of very extensive general trade. It is a fair example of the prosperous Texan city, and is one of the most important stops *en route* to San Antonio. Its location is on Buffalo Bayou, about forty-five miles from the point where it enters the Galveston Bay; as a situation, both from a scenic and healthful standpoint, it is considered unrivaled in the State, and has been largely resorted to by invalids. It enjoys a large trade in cotton and sugar.

GALVESTON, TEX.

2110 miles from New York. 53 miles from Houston.

Seven hours will be taken to visit this chief city of Texas, which is built on an island thirty miles long and three miles wide, separating the harbor from the Gulf of Mexico. Viewing the beautiful public buildings and picturesque environments will profitably employ the time, for it carries on one of the largest trades in the South, and its harbor is always filled with sailcraft and steamer from points all over the world. Its beach, public buildings, its parks and suburbs may all be visited in the time allowed.

SAN ANTONIO, TEX.

2372 miles from New York. 262 miles from Galveston.

Six hours is the stop at San Antonio, and the tourist's attention will be thoroughly occupied in that time with the numerous points of interest.

One noted shrine, to which all immediately direct their steps, is the Alamo, directly in the centre of the city. As far back as 1698 a handful of Franciscan monks, to avoid the encroachments of the French under the pretensions of La Salle, removed their tiny settlement from the Rio Grande to the mission of San Antonio de Valero. The settlement embraced the church, a fort, storehouses, dormitories of the friars and huts of the laborers, all inclosed behind a stone wall, which made a formidable fortress against the incursions of the Indians. Could the walls of the old fort tell their actual story, and the church, what thrilling and heartrending privations it played an active part in, 'twould reveal a history of such interest and feeling the like of which would be very hard to equal. It was at the Alamo that the renowned defense was made by Travis, Borne, Evans, and Davy Crockett with one hundred and forty-four men, against Santa Ana with fifteen hundred picked soldiers from the Mexican army, who, being goaded on from shell behind, at last scaled the walls and butchered the starving besieged. The entire town had capitulated at promise of mercy and speedy release. but the word of Santa Ana was as uncertain and false as chaff in a wind. Four hundred and twelve prisoners, including the garrison, one Palm Sunday morning, were brought out in single file and shot down like dogs.

The ruins of the Alamo are standing, and many a heart and eye are full when reading the eloquence graved on the marking "shaft." "Thermopylæ had its messenger of defeat—the Alamo had none!"

Government Hill, one of the finest military posts in America, should be visited; it is easily reached, and abounds in interest. A visit to these points, as well as the modern buildings on the west side of the Alamo Plaza, will pretty thoroughly occupy the time of the tourist in this ancient American town.

TORREON, MEX.

2924 miles from New York.   383 miles from Eagle Pass.   552 miles from San Antonio.
706 miles to City of Mexico.

As a railroad junction point is chiefly notable.   It is also a commercial centre of some importance as the shipping point for the vast cotton, sugar cane, corn, and wheat growths of the outlying fields.   The stop here occupies but an hour and a half, yet in that time sufficient of interest may be seen to warrant a little excursion by foot from the train about the town.

ZACATECAS, MEX.

3191 miles from New York.   267 miles from Torreon.   439 miles from City of Mexico.

This city of the clouds is eight thousand two hundred and sixty-five feet above sea level, despite the fact of its being located in the bottom of a picturesque valley. Long before its towers and cathedral domes, like white sentinels, raise their heads above the horizon, Nature discloses to her lovers scenery as grand and overpowering as the cañons of Colorado. Excitement coupled with wonder are the prevailing sensations as the marvelous revelations of nineteenth century engineering skill pass in review during the run of nine miles between Calera and Zacatecas. Standing boldly above the

A STREET SCENE AT MARKET HOUR.

city is the Bufa (Buffalo), a mountain ridge rising five hundred feet above the principal park of the city. From its height on the threshold of the old shrine of the pilgrimages, the Chapel of Los Remidios, built in 1728, is commanded a view warranting any exertion to enjoy.

The city derives its importance and wealth from the silver mines, as it is the figurative heart centre of all mining operations in the State of which it is the capital. It was founded as early as 1548, and its rapid increase in wealth and influence was the cause of a royal order being issued in 1585 by Philip II. of Spain, making it a city.

Its people belong to the ancient Mexican type, proudly maintaining their old customs and costumes, and presenting strange and quaint sights nowhere else found in Mexico. The Government buildings are very fine structures, but the churches and cathedrals here, as in almost every Mexican city of age, show the lavish expenditure of money. The Grand Cathedral, commenced in 1612, dedicated in 1752, and consecrated in 1864, is of magnificent proportions and beautifully decorated, its interior being of pure white and gold. A half dozen other churches, all dating from the seventeenth century, possess rare interest for the tourist. The mint is well worth a visit, as also the public park, squares, and mines, while a visit to Zacatecas could not be counted complete if the omission of a side trip to Guadalupe was recorded against one. The distance to this beautiful park and garden town is but five miles, connected by a tramway descending by force of gravity and returning by the primitive force of mule power.

AGUASCALIENTES, MEX.

3266 miles from New York. 75 miles from Zacatecas. 364 miles from City of Mexico.

Here are located the famous hot springs, from which the place takes name, and the city holds the reputation of being one of the most attractive places in the Republic, and certainly is destined to become one of the greatest health resorts of the world. To the left of the railway station are the *aguas calientes*, or warm-water baths heated by Nature's own furnace. In the town proper is a very pretentious bathing establishment called the *Baños Chicos*, where these same waters may be used, as they are conducted thence in pipes. Here may be seen the dilapidated Church of *Neustro Señor de Los Encinos*, wherein are some fourteen life-size paintings by Lopez. A recent writer describes the baths used by the inhabitants thus :—

" Along the whole length of the canal or sluiceway, as far as the eye can reach, are scattered hundreds of natives, of both sexes and all ages, lining the water's edge and disporting themselves in every conceivable state of *deshabille*. In fact, it might as well be stated that the assemblage is divided into two classes, those who have something on and those who have nothing—five hundred of the descendants of Montezuma quietly taking their baths at high noon, on a public highway, with only such privacy as the Republic of Mexico and the blue sky of heaven afford !"

LEON, MEX.

3371 miles from New York. 105 miles from Aguascalientes. 258 miles from
City of Mexico.

Leon is a place of one hundred thousand inhabitants, and is one of the greatest manufacturing towns in the republic. Its situation, like Torreon, is in the midst of rich grazing lands and highly cultivated farms hedged by gigantic cactus of the tree or organ variety—so-called on account of its resemblance to the pipes of an organ, and which is a feature of every Mexican landscape. Leon as a place is exceedingly quaint, with narrow, irregularly-angled streets, and curious homes and houses. There are the workshops of the leather-dressers and where the noted saddles are finished. Aside from the manufacturing interest there is a pretty plaza, where after the business hours the inhabitants congregate as one family enjoying their music and cooling drinks.

SILAO, MEX.

3392 miles from New York. 21 miles from Leon. 238 miles from City of Mexico.

Silao has about fifteen thousand inhabitants ; it is very pleasantly built in a picturesque section of the country. There is quite a large English-speaking population, due principally to its being the headquarters, or a divisional point of the railway, and within comparatively short distance from the City of Mexico. It is at Silao that another branch of the Mexican Central Railway connects Marfil and Guanajuato, a city of one hundred thousand inhabitants. This now quiet and picturesque town was only a few years back the headquarters of the noted Mexican banditti, and the term " After Dark in Silao " even now quiets the bad child and suggests the daring deeds of the far-famed robbers.

GUANAJUATO, MEX.

3407 miles from New York. 15 miles from Silao. 253 miles from the City of Mexico.

This remarkably old point is reached by a branch line from Silao, and the run thither is very picturesque, winding around among the hills,

STREET SCENE AND CATHEDRAL, GUANAJUATO.

where there are some pretty fields, passing adobe villages, and coming to Marfil. From here on a horse-car line is taken, which goes at a gallop up the barranca, passing some of the greatest silver mines of the world and the haciendas where the reduction works are located, for this settlement divides distinction with Zacatecas as an important mining town. The street, or road, along which the cars pass is crowded with people going to and fro, and with burros loaded with silver ore. The hills rise up high and steep on both sides, and wherever there is a place large enough in the rocks a house is built, the method of getting up or down being a secondary consideration ; and how the feat is accomplished by any animal short of a goat, or by any other means than a hook and ladder outfit, nobody will be able to determine. The homes of these cliff-dwellers dot the hills on both sides of the barranca and around the city.

The curious graveyard on the crest of the hill will be of great interest to the tourist. Here the allotted grave space is rented out, similar to the temporary possession of a post-office box, and if by ill-luck arrears in dues occur the remains of the occupant are scattered to the four winds. After three miles of this Moorish street travel the cars stop at a charming little plaza, adorned with flowers and tropical plants. Here are the hotels and the centre of the city. The end of the track is opposite a lovely little park at the head of the ravine. This is the Alameda, and above it is the reservoir of the city's water supply. Several attractive residences are perched on the mountain-side, with a towering cliff at their back doors and miniature lakes at the front, while gallery and casement are hung with brightest flowers. There is no such street nor such houses even in Mexico capital.

Looking across a reservoir of clear water may be seen little low houses of Pompeiian colors with case-mated windows covered with flowering vines, the gable toward the water,

A BURRO TEAM.

with an old wheel window, around which the vines climb. On a wall mayhap stands a peacock with feathers outspread 'gainst a light background, whilst the other birds sit quietly as if posing for a picture. Ducks swim lazily in the water of the foreground. The bridge thrown across the water is shaded by trees of japonica with bright yellow flowers growing through all their branches, making a truly ideal picture.

QUERETARO, MEX.

3507 miles from New York. 100 miles from Guanajuato. 153 miles from the
City of Mexico.

This is the particular point the tourist has looked for, not only on account of its opal mines, its stupendous aqueduct, its interesting churches, and its celebrated factories, but because it is here the sad short reigning life of Maximilian may be viewed from his triumphant entry into the country until he was taken out and shot on the little barren hill in the suburbs of Queretaro.

The town is of very ancient origin, having been founded by the Aztecs about 1445, and conquered by the Spaniards in July, 1531, led by a Lieutenant Cortez. In 1655 it was created by the King of Spain a city, and is historically of the greatest interest. Prominent notable events in its modern life were the ratification of the treaty of peace with the United States in 1848, its defense by Maximilian against the Liberal forces under General Escobedo, its fall, and the execution of Maximilian, Mejia, and Miramon in 1867. It is bathed perpetually in a tropical atmosphere, with products of summer at command all the year round. It is the reputed Conservative town of Mexico, and the tower of defense of the church party.

CITY OF MEXICO, MEX.

3660 miles from New York. 1119 miles from Eagle Pass. 143 miles from Queretaro.

It was Bayard Taylor who pronounced the City of Mexico one of the loveliest scenes of the civilized world. Reading on the subject ever fails to give any impression like that of the reality.

This beautiful city is built upon ground that was once the bed of a great lake. By reason of its population, intelligence, culture, beautiful location, healthful and even climate, historical, political, and commercial pre-eminence, it is justly entitled to its reputation as one of the celebrated cities of the world. It is well lighted, supplied with pure water, has a police force uniformly efficient ; abundance of public carriages at reasonable rates, under careful city regulations ; fine hotels, restaurants, cafés, gardens, baths, theatres, public library, museums, art galleries, and fine public buildings. Its colleges and schools are large and thoroughly organized. The National Palace, the City Hall, the great Cathedral and many of the churches are grand in architectural proportions and artistic effects. The suburbs are attractive and connected by tramways. In about twelve hours one can reach the eternal snows of the summit of Popocatapetl, or the tropical heat and fruits of the "tierra caliente."

More than three hundred years ago Hernando Cortez left Texcoco, climbed the eastern hills beyond the lake, and looked across the waters on the temple Tenochitlan ; he gazed with no less wonder than the peaceful invaders of to-day who come through the Tajo de Nochistongo, and see from Huehuetoca the towers of the City of Mexico, now built where stood the temples of Tenochitlan. In 1519 that ancient Aztec city was in the midst of the plain where Mexico's capital is, and the chief temple stood on the present Cathedral's site. When Cortez came it was after a very wearisome journey from the coast. Montezuma met his guest at the causeways, and with a special committee of a hundred thousand warriors; the reception to-day is, perhaps, less imposing, but none the less truly welcome, from something less than a hundred thousand *cocheros*, who, with their green flags and blue, red flags and white, stand ready to receive the coming man to Mexico at a price indicated by the colors displayed on their *coches;* they form a committee of hack-

THE CATHEDRAL.

men in body. There is a difference in favor of the Mexican "cabby," in that you do not have to ask the rate of fare, even if you know how. Each vehicle carries a small tin flag about four by two inches, which must always be nailed to the mast unless engaged.

These flags indicate the class of vehicle and the tariff. Those with a green flag make a rate of $1.50 per hour or 75 cents per single passenger for a short drive within a district ; the blue flag hires for $1 by the hour or 50 cents per passenger ; the red, 75 cents per hour or 25 cents per passenger ; the white flags are the cheapest, being only 50 cents per hour or whatever the passenger will pay, and if the red or white flags are selected, it is purely from an economical point of view, with no pretense to style of rig, and with no particular desire as to when the destination is to be reached. If overcharges are made, and Mexican hackmen are not unlike their American brethren, ask for their number, *numero* is the word to use, and he will usually lapse to tariff rates. If a carriage is wanted for a single trip, simply call the name of the place ; if by the hour, say "*por hora*," and the prices will be given, green flags, *un peso y cuatro reales ;* " blue, "*un peso ;* " red, "*seis reales ;* " white, "*cuatro reales*." After dark, figures are increased 75 cents for white.

and on feast days and Sundays, these to $2, green ; $1.50, blue ; $1, red ; and It is easy to find one's way about the city, and the fact that all prominent horse-car lines start from and return to the Plaza Mayor, in front of the Cathedral, makes confusion impossible.

The street-car system in the City of Mexico is a good one, reaching all railway stations and nearly every point of interest in and around the city. Fares in the city *un medio* (6¼ cents), to the suburbs *un real* (12½ cents), and *dos reales* (25 cents), according to the distance traveled. The second-class cars are much cheap-

CHURCH OF LA SANTISSIMA, CITY OF MEXICO.

er, but are only patronized by the poorer classes. They are painted green and follow a half block behind the first-class cars, which are painted yellow. Parties desiring to visit points of interest may hire a special car as one would a carriage, for the afternoon or all day.

The horse-car driver carries a tin horn, not unlike the campaign horn of the United States, which he blows assiduously, as a note of warning at street intersections. Conductors sell tickets and a collector gets on the cars at certain points of the route and takes them up.

The street-car companies do not confine their operations to the passenger business solely, doing a large freight business as well.

Cars leave the Plaza Mayor at short intervals of from fifteen to thirty minutes morning and afternoon, and less frequently in the evening, when the fares are increased.

Nearly all the points of interest in and around the city may be more conveniently, comfortably, and quickly reached by car than by carriage.

The principal points of visiting interest are the Cathedral, El Placio del poder Ejecutivo de la Nacion, or the White House, Colegro Minerea,

WAITING FOR THE MARKET BOATS, LA VIGA CANAL.

El Musea Nacional, El Conservatorio de Musica, La Academia de San Carlos, La Biblioteca Nacional, and El Aqueducto.

SUBURBS OF THE CITY OF MEXICO.

Among the suburban points of interest are the gardens and orchards of San Angel and Tacubaya, a place of summer resort of the native upper crust, and sort of local Monte Carlo. A line of cars goes very near to the Castle of Chapultepec, but from thence a closer view necessitates a tiresome walk up the hill; it is best to take a carriage to Chapultepec. Popotla, Tacuba, and Atzcapotzalco are, also, the destinations of horse-car tours that are most interesting. On the line to Tacuba, which was once a causeway, is the place of *"el salto de Alvarado"* (the leap of Alvarado), where that warrior made his famous leap for life. The exact spot, as shown, is in front of the *Tivoli del Eliseo*. At the end of the causeway, near the church of San Estèban, is the tree of *Noche Triste* (the dismal night), where Cortez sat down and cried after his defeat. The tree is a giant *ahuehuete* or cypress, of great age, now inclosed with an iron rail to prevent a recurrence of further vandalism, as occurred some years ago, by a crank having set it on fire.

The floating gardens, *Chinampas*, on the Viga canal, are reached by horse-cars from the Plaza Mayor, near the Cathedral, to Embarcadero, and thence by canoe. The boats are a sort of a Mexican edition of a Venetian gondola, broad and flat-bottomed, with seats underneath a canopy in bright colors; they are propelled by a pole in the hands of a dusky native. The excursion is altogether a novel one, particularly on Sundays and feast days, and will not be overlooked. Unless you are thoroughly Mexican it is best to make a picnic of it and take your provender along, but as you are gliding along there will come alongside a longer and narrower

A NATIVE GONDOLIER.

canoe hewn from the trunk of a single tree. In one end of this quaint craft stands a swarthy Mexican with a single oar of long handle—in the other a comely woman and often a pretty girl, who will offer for a *tlaco* or a *cuartilla*, the native sandwich, a *tortilla con carne* or a *tortilla con dulce*. No advice is given as to this purchase, but the tortillas of La Viga will be found clean and toothsome.

This excursion is indeed a novel one. The boatmen meet the horse-cars at the terminus and bid against each other for patronage; there is no regular tariff, twenty-five cents (*dos reales*) for each passenger is sufficient to Santa Anita and return; the longer excursions to the lakes and towns beyond, of course, cost more. Santa Anita is a sort of native Coney Island, and is a great resort, but the charm is in the ride thither, passing under the low-arched bridges, the market boats laden with fruits and flowers, which must stop at the La Viga gate and pay a duty to the city, levied on all imports from the country. There are great, long, flat-bottomed passenger packets, also propelled by poles, going to and from the towns across on the other shores of Texcoco, Xochimilco, and Chalco, crowded with men, women, and children and dogs, starting or returning from a voyage of a day and a night.

Any day will do for the La Viga voyage; but Sunday, or, better still, on a feast day, there will be flowers afloat and ashore, and music of every description, most of it in harmony, from the tinkle of a guitar to the blare of a brass band; gayly dressed men and more gayly dressed women, singing and dancing on the boats or under the trees of the Paseo de La Viga, which is a walk extending along the canal. On the banks of La Viga once lived El Señor Don Juan Corona of most happy memory, revered for deeds of daring, and loved for his charity; he was not a soldier nor a Sunday-school superintendent; in life Don Juan was a bull fighter, the much renowned in his day. The gondolier will stop at the hacienda of Don Juan Corona. Entering beneath a hospitable roof one will find a house intensely Mexican, shaded by trees and almost hidden by climbing vines and flowers. Every room is a museum in itself, filled with relics of every age and time of Mexico's history, curious objects collected from all over the country, in dozens and scores; there is a cigar-case once owned by the patriot priest Hidalgo,

UNLOADING THE MARKET BOATS, LA VIGA CANAL.

also a pistol and sword carried by him; some pieces from the table service of the Emperor Maximilian; several idols found in the pyramids of San Juan Teotihuacan; weapons, feathers, and war-dresses used by the Aztecs; one of the guns with which Maximilian was shot; the bed used by General Santa Ana, while president of Mexico; a rifle used by General Miramon in the siege of Queretaro; a magnificent collection of *chicaras* (chocolate cups) painted by the Indians of the State of Michoacan; very curious ancient bull-fighter dresses, among which is the one used by the Spanish matador Bernardo Gaviño when he was killed in the ring at Texcoco.

GUADALUPE CHURCH.

The church of Guadalupe, commandingly perched on the crown of a high hill, is at the end of a most interesting horse-car excursion. Cars leave the Plaza Mayor half hourly, and run through the narrow streets, cross the marshes on a broad causeway lined with trees—in ancient times of practical road use, but now only a romantic walk. Many shrines along the route are still standing, and here the people stop to invoke the blessing of this saint or that as the pilgrimage moves on to the holiest shrine.

There are churches and pictures in Mexico, but Guadalupe is the holiest shrine of all and has the most mysterious picture—a representation of the Virgin—which, although nearly four hundred years old and appearing on an Indian *tilma* of the cheapest, commonest sort, and during these three centuries has been exposed to a salty deteriorating air, its colors are bright and fresh as if painted yesterday; and in proof of its alleged divine origin the decay of surrounding pictures is pointed out, while this remains alone fresh and bright. Legend says that a pious Indian, *Juan Diego* by name, was surprised by an apparition of the Virgin, who commanded him to gather flowers on the barren hill where she appeared and where the church now stands. To gather flowers in such a place seemed impossible, but he found them there, gathered them in his *tilma* and carried them to the priest with the message that a shrine to the Virgin must be erected on the spot. The Indian's story was not believed, but when the flowers were emptied from his *tilma* there appeared a most perfect picture of the Virgin, in style different from any other, and painted in such colors that even the artists of to-day have not been able to fathom their ingredients or the mysterious laying on. The church was built as it stands to-day, and over its altar, in a frame of gold, hangs the *tilma* with the sacred picture. A fund of some millions of dollars has been collected to provide a surmounting crown of gold, but it now waits the sanction of the powers at Rome before the plan can be carried out.

The cars stop at the foot of the hill, crowning which is the shrine of Guadalupe. Passing through a little garden or park to the right of the church, one comes to a small chapel, in the entrance of which is a fountain of pure, clear water, which is said to have gushed forth from the ground where the Virgin stood when she appeared to Juan Diego. From this spot around the corner of a narrow street are some stone stairs leading to the shrine or chapel on the crest of the hill where Juan gathered the flowers, and is one of the most picturesque localities in all Mexico. On ascending the stairs may be seen, on the

GARDEN OF MAXIMILIAN PALACE.

right near the top, what seems to be a ship's mast with sails all set, done in stone. A legend says that some storm-tossed sailors prayed to the Virgin of Guadalupe and vowed that if they were saved from a watery grave they would carry the mast to the shrine and erect it there as a memorial and thank-offering—which 'tis said they did carry from Vera Cruz, incased it in stone, and erected it where it stands to-day.

CASTLE OF CHAPULTEPEC.

This castle occupies a noble position upon the summit of a rocky hill which lifts itself considerably above the neighboring plain, and is surrounded by a magnificent grove of old cypress trees, from which depend festoons of Spanish moss. There are walks and drives through the grove, and at the foot of the hill is the spring from whence the city derives its chief water supply, and also a monument to the cadets who fell in defense of the castle when it was attacked by the Americans in 1847. The castle occupies the site of Montezuma's palace. In rear of the hill is the ground where the sanguinary battle of Molino del Rey was fought at the time of the storming of the castle. A portion of the structure has been fitted up as a residence for President Diaz and his successors, and the rest is occupied as the National Military School. There are about three hundred and twenty cadets, the full complement of the school, at the present time. The view from the ramparts and terraces is magnificent, comprising the city, with its many domes and towers, the surrounding fields and meadows, and the inclosing mountains, with Popocatapetl and Ixtaccihuatl standing proudly above all.

ESPERANZA, MEX.

3812 miles from New York. 152 miles from the City of Mexico.

Esperanza is a great shipping point for cereals, ores, and other products of the country, brought here on burros to be forwarded on the cars ; all about the station the burros may be seen forming picturesque groups as they stand lazily waiting to unload or start on the return trip.

ORIZABA, MEX.

3841 miles from New York. 29 miles from Esperanza.
181 miles from City of Mexico.

THE PEAK AT ORIZABA.

This city, nestling in a lovely valley, is inhabited by twenty thousand people. It is a town quaintly picturesque, and is located just on the border of the hot country. It is said to occupy the site of an ancient town conquered by Montezuma in the fifteenth century. Tourists will have an advantage by starting early on their investigation trips, and here there is much to see : the old churches, the plaza, the alameda with its tropical flowers, the market places, the bull-fighting arena, which is in an old convent, the waterfalls in the neighborhood, and all the great natural beauty of the place proper and suburbs.

On the left, overlooking the city, is the hill where a sharp battle was fought between the French and Mexicans, and a cross is erected there to the memory of the fallen. This great Mount of Orizaba, as illustrated herein, was known by the ancients as the "Mountain of the Star," and tradition tells us that the "God of the Air" was

THE CATHEDRAL.

buried in its peak, consumed by fire and then took flight to the higher realm in the disguise of a peacock.

PASO DEL MACHO, MEX.

3876 miles from New York. 35 miles from Orizaba. 216 miles from City of Mexico.

This settlement is the extreme southern point touched by the tour.

SANTA ANA, MEX.

3946 miles from New York. 105 miles from Orizaba. 96 miles from City of Mexico.

Santa Ana in itself would consume the time devoted to the stop, but the disposition of the short stay must be divided to the sight-seeing in and about the town. It is a station on the line leading from Apizaco to Puebla, and though not occupied as extensively as many of its sister settlements in manufacture it presents an antique and historical life of great interest. It also holds an important railroad position.

TLAXCALA, MEX.

Tlaxcala is reached from Santa Ana by tramway. It is the capital of the State of same name and is one of the gray-bearded cities of Mexico, holding invaluable relics. The Tlaxcalans at the time of Cortez's conquest numbered some forty thousand and aided materially in accomplishing Montezuma's overthrow ; to-day difficulty would be encountered in gathering one-tenth that number. Paintings, the Cortez banner, and old Indian and Spanish relics will interest the tourist and afford those with cameras ample opportunity for snap shots. The Convent of San Francisco dating back to the sixteenth century is the first of four religious establishments of its kind built by the Spanish fathers. In it are many paintings, and the first pulpit erected in the new world.

CHOLULA, MEX.

Cholula is chiefly noted for its famous ancient monument, the Aztec Pyramid.

This handsome structure was first built over two hundred feet high on the crest of the height, and was the dedicated temple to Quetzalocatl, "God of Air," but now it is changed into a church. A paved road winds up the side of the hill to the pyramid and a beautiful command of the surrounding views of far-off hills, volcanoes, and valley is obtained, while directly at the hill's base spreads the quaint little village of Cholula. This relic of the ancients is two hundred and four feet in height, measures one thousand and sixty feet at the base, and its top is a platform one hundred and sixty-five feet square. It is composed of alternate strata of brick and clay. The sides are now overgrown with grass, shrubs, and even large trees. The view at the top of this winding road is surpassingly beautiful. Popocatapetl is not more than twenty miles distant, and is visible from its base to its snow-covered summit, as well as the long, snow-capped ridge of Ixtaccihuatl. In the opposite direction rises the black mass of Malinche; and in the distance, to the right of Puebla, is the great snow cone of Orizaba. Cholula is spread out at the foot of the pyramid, its plaza and neighboring churches being prominent objects; and all around are rich fields of corn and wheat. Scattered everywhere about the fair plain are little villages, with church towers, or else churches standing alone, while their morning or curfew bells vibratingly chant their religious tones, far and near.

AZTEC PYRAMID.

PUEBLA, MEX.

Puebla is not behind the average American city; horse-cars lead to all parts of the city and to the surrounding villages, making it quite a railway centre. It is located seven thousand one hundred feet above the sea level, is an important manufacturing and mercantile point, and a marvelously beautiful place with its many streets and houses decorated with glazed tiles. The twin volcanoes are nearer to Puebla than they are to the City of Mexico, and the view is as equally fine.

Puebla was founded in 1531, and retains many

CHURCH OF SAN CRISTOBAL, PUEBLA.

of its old Spanish characteristics. The use in the city of richly colored glazed tiles produces the most beautiful effects. Not alone upon the domes and outer and inner walls of churches are these tiles used, but for exterior and interior decoration of a majority of the houses. The city was formerly called *Puebla de los Angeles:* but since the victorious battle of the Mexicans against the French, which was fought on the neighboring heights of Loreto and Guadalupe, May 5th, 1862, under the direction of General Ignacio Zaragoza, it has borne the title of *Puebla de Zaragoza.* A cathedral occupies the southern side of the *Plaza Mayor*, and is

BEGGARS.

a magnificent edifice with a dome and two high towers, from which a magnificent view is to be had of the rich valley below and the great snow-crowned peaks of the three mountains. The churches of La Compania, Nuestra Senora del Carmen, and San Francisco warrant a visit, and the market place is not without interest.

GUADALAJARA, MEX.

4460 miles from New York. 495 miles from Puebla. 380 miles from City of Mexico.

Guadalajara is a very beautiful and very interesting city, the capital of Jalisco. For centuries it has been noted for its fine pottery, ornamental and glazed, in the most beautiful and fantastic designs. Manufacturing in almost every branch is carried on, as this has for centuries been a great commercial centre and distributing point for a large territory. There are four lines of horse-railways leading to the different suburbs, each one offering something of interest to the tourist.

The city is beautifully laid out ; the streets run at right angles and for many blocks the walk-ways are under the stone *portales*. There are no finer public buildings anywhere in Mexico than in Guadalajara. Among these are the Cathedral, the Governor's palace, and the Degollado theatre, all magnificent specimens of the Mexican style of architecture, and of such proportions as to be totally unexpected in this far-away region so long without communication with the outside world.

Through the eastern part of the city runs the San Juan de Dios, and along that stream is the paseo from the alameda to the southern boundary of the city. The *Alameda, Plaza de Armas, Jardin Botanico, Parque Alcade, and Calzada de San Pedro* are all pretty parks or gardens where there are music and flowers—places of great resort in the evening, Sundays, and feast days.

The Hospital of Guadalajara contains twenty-three patios, and each has its flowers, plants, and fountains.

What with the markets, streets, people, and scenery, the tourists will have their hands full in reviewing.

THE FALLS OF JUANACATLAN, MEX.

This Mexican Niagara is about fifteen miles from Guadalajara. The Rio Lerma where the water makes its desperate plunge has a width of about six hundred feet, and the falls have a sheer descent of nearly seventy feet. It is one of the most picturesque sights in Mexico. Surely it is a weak rival to America's great boast, yet it resembles the Niagara River's leap, in miniature.

Waterfalls are not common in Mexico at all seasons. It is only in the rainy season, when water falls to any alarming extent; then there are cascades and cataracts that are not all in your eye, so to speak; they are here, there, and everywhere, and are not always either useful or ornamental—but Juanacatlan is a beauty and a joy forever in Mexico in that its waters flow on forever, in season or out of season, and the journey thither is one of the tourist's things to do.

CHIHUAHUA, MEX.

5401 miles from New York. 941 miles from Guadalajara. 999 miles from City of Mexico.

The city of Chihuahua, capital of the State of Chihuahua, was founded in 1539, and is built upon a high plain four thousand six hundred feet above the sea, surrounded by mountains, giving it the salubrious climate for which it is famed. The centre of attraction in the city is the Cathedral, of whose beauty and magnificence so much has been written. It is a grand and stately pile of light-colored stone, with an immense central dome and two lofty towers. The facade of the Cathedral is embellished with life-size statues of the Saviour and the twelve Apostles, while the interior is ornamented with many fine paintings. The towers contain many bells, one of which was shattered by a cannon ball from the invading army of Maximilian in 1866. These bells of the Cathedral are very mellow-toned. From these towers an extended view of the attractive valley can be obtained. The Cathedral was built in the early part of the last century at a cost of $800,000. It is second only in size to the grand Cathedral in Mexico City, and is, without doubt, the noblest structure in Northern Mexico.

A visit to the Mint is not without reward, for, aside from the usual attractions of an institution of that kind, visitors are shown the tower room in which Miguel Hidalgo, the Liberator priest of Mexico, who led the Revolution of 1810, was confined the night previous to his execution, July 31st, 1811. A monument now marks the spot where he was executed.

Other buildings of note are the State House, Convent of San Francisco, Mexico National Bank, Bank of Santa Eulalia, several theatres and hotels, and last, but not least, the market, which should not be neglected, for it is here that the Northern tourist will find fruits peculiar to this section of the world, unknown in the Northern and Eastern States.

The city has several charming parks liberally supplied with seats of stone and masonry, under grand old shade trees ; and with the perfume of flowering shrubs and plants, the tinkling waters of the fountains and strains of sweet Mexican music, one does not wonder that the whole city turns out at evening to enjoy itself in these lovely spots.

At the Chapel of Guadalupe, which stands at the head of one of the parks, may be seen a statue of Loyola, the great Jesuit, and just beyond an attractive avenue leading into one of the fashionable suburbs of the city, containing a number of fine houses and beautifully-kept gardens. The Rio Chubisco, a pretty stream, runs through the city and adds much to the beauty of Chihuahua. The city is supplied with pure water, which is brought a distance of three and a half miles by an immense aqueduct built on arches of stone and constructed over two hundred years ago. It is a truly wonderful piece of masonry, and travelers are impressed with its resemblance to the remnants of the Claudian aqueduct which crossed the Campagna at Rome.

Tourists will be impressed with the commercial activity of the city. The machine shops and foundry of the Compañia Industrial Mexicana, on such a large scale, suggest the enterprise of a manufacturing city in the United States.

The inexhaustible silver mines of the surrounding mountains have contributed to the wealth and importance of the city. A visit to some of these mines, and listening to the romantic history of their discovery and early workings as told by the miners, will amply repay the time. The Santa Eulalia Mine, only one of the many which surround Chihuahua, has been worked for several hundred years, and it alone, between 1703 and 1833, yielded silver to the amount of $344,000,000. There are some wonderful and only partly-explored caves in the vicinity of Chihuahua, which are claimed to be more beautiful in stalactite and stalagmite formations than the Mammoth Cave of Kentucky.

A great attraction Chihuahua possesses, and which assumes the form of a monopoly, is the tiny Chihuahua dog, wonderfully small and remarkably intelligent. Its origin is enveloped in mystery, and not being found in any other part of the country renders Chihuahua the Mecca for all pet dog fanciers.

EL PASO, TEX.

The quaintness of El Paso, with its picturesqueness of situation, is strongly marked. Across the river, connected by horse-cars, lies the old town of Paso del Norte, newly named Juarez, both places, with their crooked streets, irregular roads, and sunburnt-brick houses, speaking eloquently of the Mexican. At El Paso Central time changes to Pacific. Paso del Norte is supposed to have been settled about the year 1585. In September, 1888, a monument to the memory of Benito Jaurez was unveiled, and the name of the place was changed to that of its famous son, whose patriotic deeds had won a laurel crown for his country. There is an old church at the head of the plaza. El Paso is a compact and more flourishing town, with every evidence of American thrift, energy, and enterprise. The city contains many new and handsome structures, including a county court-house, schools, churches, and business edifices.

SANTA FÉ, N. MEX.

Santa Fé is one of the oldest settlements on the American continent, and replete with interest. The Plaza, or Mud Palace, which has been the seat of every grade of government, from the barbaric to the civilized, should be visited, as well as the Cathedral and the old Church of San Miguel. Five hours of daylight will be allowed here.

LAS VEGAS HOT SPRINGS, N. MEX.

The respect of men for the mysterious fountains freshly flowing from the laboratories of the gnomes and elves, and warmed in subterranean cauldrons, extends far back into savagery. The cures effected by them are accepted facts older than medical science. These springs, more than any other locality in a wide realm of mountain and plateau, were the subjects of tradition. They were even a subject of tribal jealousy, and were guarded by painted and feathered sentinels against use or seizure by some other tribe.

COLORADO SPRINGS, COL.

2012 miles to New York. 331 miles from Las Vegas Hot Springs.

At Colorado Springs ample opportunity will be afforded to thoroughly view the charming city under the shadow of Pike's Peak. The climate is grand, and the scenic attractions unrivaled. Seven miles away is the famous resort Manitou, with its world-renowed "Garden of the Gods."

DENVER, COL.

1937 miles to New York. 75 miles from Colorado Springs.

In this pushing, bright, and cultured city of the plain, the social and commercial centre of not only Colorado alone, but of the outlying States, there is much to admire in the handiwork of man, and enough to fill with interest the eight hours to be devoted to it. Within a figurative stone's throw of its walls are the world-known cattle ranches and silver-producing sections. The industry of wresting the precious metals from their rocky prisons is carried on upon a very extensive scale and may be seen a short distance outside of the city. Denver seems to the returning traveler the portal to the populous East.

CHICAGO, ILL.

912 miles to New York. 1025 miles from Denver.

An adequate description to cover the numerous points of interest in the World's Fair City cannot be given here. However, tourists will scarcely need such an aid. The drives to the site of the Fair and a review of buildings erected so far, the visit to the parks, museums, public buildings and stock-yards will thoroughly occupy the time, and perhaps the best illustration of push, rush, and American activity in business, as seen in the Chicago streets, will be a revelation to many.

REDEMPTION OF TICKETS.

All tickets must be paid for at least one week prior to the date of departure of the tour.

If, for any reason, purchasers of tickets are unable to use them, the tickets will be redeemed, provided they are presented for redemption, either personally or by letter, at the General Office of the Company, Philadelphia, one week prior to the date of the tour.

Letters and requests for reservations of space or tickets may be addressed to Geo. W. Boyd, Assistant General Passenger Agent, Philadelphia, Pa., or to Tourist Agent, Pennsylvania Railroad, at the offices given below.

OFFICES OF THE TOURIST AGENTS OF THE COMPANY.

PHILADELPHIA . . . . 233 South Fourth Street.
NEW YORK . . . . 849 Broadway.
BOSTON . . . . 205 Washington Street.

THE STAFF OF THE TOURIST DEPARTMENT.

Tourist Agents.	*Chaperons.*
COLIN STUDDS,	MRS. H. F. BENDER,
J. P. MCWILLIAMS,	MISS E. C. BINGHAM,
THOMAS PURDY.	MISS ZERELDA W. BEATY.

☞ The importance of reserving space at once is apparent, as the tour is absolutely limited not to exceed eighty persons.

TIME-TABLES giving the schedule of the movement of the Special Trains will be placed in the hands of every tourist, so that he may see at a glance just where the train is at any hour. These tables will be forwarded to every purchaser of a ticket, and a supply of them will be placed on the train.

ADVANTAGES OF THE MEXICAN TOUR.

There can be no question as to the attractiveness of Mexico as a field for the tourist. Mythological associations linger around its ruins, while its mountains, valleys, and cities are clustered about with historical and contemporary interest. Its quaint people, their curious customs and manner of living, the houses, the churches, and even the wayside shrines, cannot fail to attract and absorb the attention of the Northern visitor. Novel scenes follow each other with the rapidity of kaleidoscopic changes, and the mind of the stranger is continually receiving new impressions. Natural scenery in all the diversity of plain, valley, mountain, and peak lends a charm to the landscape which is rendered more beautiful by flowers and shrubbery that thrive beneath a tropical sky.

It is an old land being warmed into a new life by an invigorated civilization, and while the monuments of a richly historical past are preserved with sacred care, the influence of a new spirit is clearly manifested in modern institutions and development.

The republic of Mexico is our neighbor and our friend. Her people are entering upon the enjoyment of that liberty which has so long been our birthright. As they learn more and more to value it, the reciprocal relations which are now being so auspiciously established will bind the sister nations in a neighborly union that cannot fail to be productive of the greatest benefits to both.

These considerations alone are sufficient to make this tour interesting and attractive to every American.

INDEX.

(55)

A

PENNSYLVANIA TOURS

TO THE

GOLDEN GATE.

Ɛ-

This is the title of a handsome illustrated Itinerary just issued by the Pennsylvania Railroad Company, containing full information as to how a personally-conducted tour may be pleasantly and profitably spent in *California or Mexico*. The first tour leaves New York January 13th, and speeds directly to the Pacific Coast via St. Louis, Kansas City, Las Vegas, and Santa Fé. The second tour, February 24th, runs directly to New Orleans via Cincinnati and Mammoth Cave, and thence, after the Mardi Gras festivities, to the Pacific Coast. The third and fourth, both through California tours, will

DATE PALMS, SAN DIEGO.

leave March 24th and April 20th respectively. Tourists will travel by superbly-appointed special trains of Pullman drawing-room sleeping, dining, smoking, and observation cars, under the supervision of a Tourist Agent and Chaperon. Residents of New England desiring to join these parties are afforded special facilities for taking the special train at New York and Philadelphia. The rates for the round trip are exceptionally low, and include not only all necessary traveling expenses *en route* to the Pacific Coast and return, but also side trips to attractive resorts in California, and several carriage and stage rides of interest.

ON THE BANKS OF THE HALIFAX.

JACKSONVILLE TOURS.

A series of six tours from New York, Philadelphia, Baltimore, Washington, and other principal points on the Pennsylvania System is fixed for the following dates :—

Tuesday, January 19th,
Tuesday, February 2d,
Tuesday, February 16th,
Tuesday, March 1st, 15th, and 29th, 1892.

The first five tours will admit of a visit of two ENTIRE WEEKS in the flowery State, and the returning parties will leave Jacksonville for home on the dates following :—

Thursday, February 4th and 18th,
Thursday, March 3d, 17th, and 31st, 1892.

Tickets for the sixth tour will be valid for return by regular trains until May 30th, 1892.

The period allowed is amply sufficient to admit of a thorough tour of all the interesting places in the Peninsula.

Rates for the round trip, $50.00 from New York, $48.00 from Philadelphia, and proportionate rates from other stations.

ILLUSTRATED ITINERARIES,

Containing all detailed information, as well as descriptive notes of California or Florida, may be procured by addressing Geo. W. Boyd, Assistant General Passenger Agent, Philadelphia, Pa., or Tourist Agent, Pennsylvania Railroad, 849 Broadway, New York, or 205 Washington Street, Boston.

R .

T   H
Grand F

k R . R.

O   T
Edgelove

Montreal

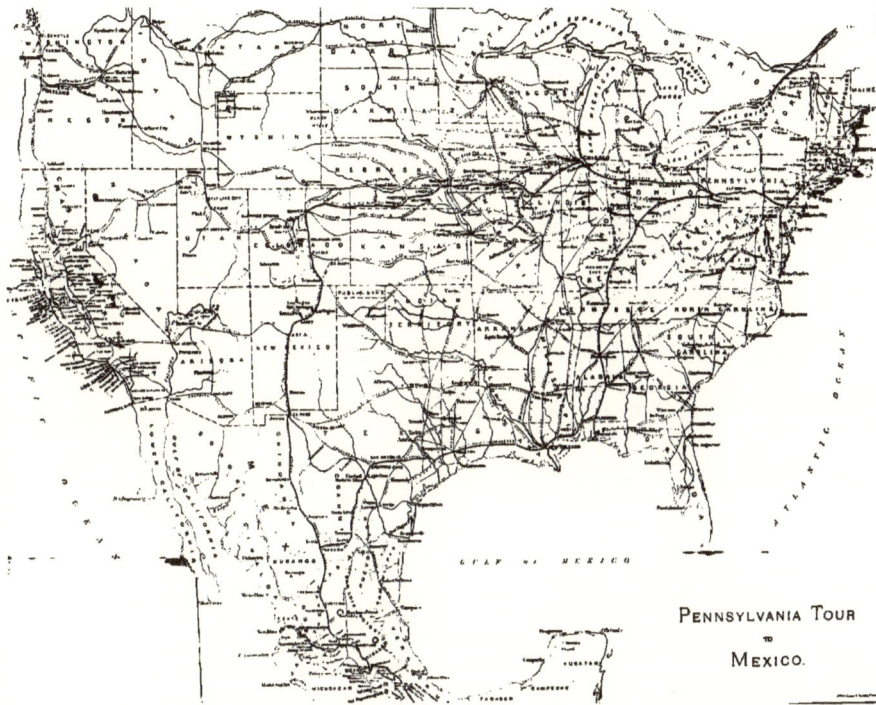

PENNSYLVANIA TOUR
TO
MEXICO.

www.ingramcontent.com/pod-product-compliance
Lightning Source LLC
Chambersburg PA
CBHW030719110426
42739CB00030B/851